W9-CBM-909

THE **MAKING** OF THE **MODERN WORLD**

Education, Poverty, and Inequality

BOOKS IN THE SERIES

THE MAKING OF THE MODERN WORLD

1945 TO THE PRESENT

Education, Poverty, and Inequality

John Perritano

SERIES ADVISOR
Ruud van Dijk

Mason Crest

Mason Crest
450 Parkway Drive, Suite D
Broomall, PA 19008
www.masoncrest.com

Produced and developed by MTM Publishing.
www.mtmpublishing.com

President and Project Coordinator: Valerie Tomaselli
Designer: Sherry Williams, Oxygen Design Group
Copyeditor: Lee Motteler, GeoMap Corp.
Editorial Coordinator: Andrea St. Aubin
Proofreader: Peter Jaskowiak

ISBN: 978-1-4222-3636-9
Series ISBN: 978-1-4222-3634-5
Ebook ISBN: 978-1-4222-8280-9

Library of Congress Cataloging-in-Publication Data

Names: Perritano, John, author.
Title: Education, poverty, and inequality / by John Perritano.
Description: Broomall, PA : Mason Crest, [2017] | Series: The making of the
    modern world: 1945 to the present | Includes index.
Identifiers: LCCN 2016006862| ISBN 9781422236369 (hardback) | ISBN
    9781422236345 (series) | ISBN 9781422282809 (ebook)
Subjects: LCSH: Economic history--1945---Juvenile literature. | Social
    history--1945---Juvenile literature. | Equality--History--Juvenile
    literature. | Developing countries--Economic conditions--Juvenile
    literature. | Developing countries--Social conditions--Juvenile
    literature. | Developing countries--Foreign relations--Juvenile literature.
Classification: LCC HC59 .P437 2017 | DDC 330.9172/4--dc23
LC record available at https://lccn.loc.gov/2016006862

Printed and bound in the United States of America.

First printing
9 8 7 6 5 4 3 2 1

QR CODES AND LINKS TO THIRD PARTY CONTENT

Contents

KEY ICONS TO LOOK FOR:

Words to understand: These words with their easy-to-understand definitions will increase the reader's understanding of the text while building vocabulary skills.

Sidebars: This boxed material within the main text allows readers to build knowledge, gain insights, explore possibilities, and broaden their perspectives by weaving together additional information to provide realistic and holistic perspectives.

Educational Videos: Readers can view videos by scanning our QR codes, providing them with additional educational content to supplement the text. Examples include news coverage, moments in history, speeches, iconic sports moments and much more!

Text-dependent questions: These questions send the reader back to the text for more careful attention to the evidence presented there.

Research projects: Readers are pointed toward areas of further inquiry connected to each chapter. Suggestions are provided for projects that encourage deeper research and analysis.

Series Introduction

In 1945, at the end of World War II, the world had to start afresh in many ways. The war had affected the entire world, destroying cities, sometimes entire regions, and killing millions. At the end of the war, millions more were displaced or on the move, while hunger, disease, and poverty threatened survivors everywhere the war had been fought.

Politically, the old, European-dominated order had been discredited. Western European democracies had failed to stop Hitler, and in Asia they had been powerless against imperial Japan. The autocratic, militaristic Axis powers had been defeated. But their victory was achieved primarily through the efforts of the Soviet Union—a communist dictatorship—and the United States, which was the only democracy powerful enough to aid Great Britain and the other Allied powers in defeating the Axis onslaught. With the European colonial powers weakened, the populations of their respective empires now demanded their independence.

The war had truly been a global catastrophe. It underlined the extent to which peoples and countries around the world were interconnected and interdependent. However, the search for shared approaches to major, global challenges in the postwar world—symbolized by the founding of the United Nations—was soon overshadowed by the Cold War. The leading powers in this contest, the United States and the Soviet Union, represented mutually exclusive visions for the postwar world. The Soviet Union advocated collectivism, centrally planned economies, and a leading role for the Communist Party. The United States sought to promote liberal democracy, symbolized by free markets and open political systems. Each believed fervently in the promise and justice of its vision for the future. And neither thought it could compromise on what it considered vital interests. Both were concerned about whose influence would dominate Europe, for example, and to whom newly independent nations in the non-Western world would pledge their allegiance. As a result, the postwar world would be far from peaceful.

As the Cold War proceeded, peoples living beyond the Western world and outside the control of the Soviet Union began to find their voices. Driven by decolonization, the developing world, or so-called Third World, took on a new importance. In particular, countries in these areas were potential allies on both sides of the Cold War. As the newly independent peoples established their own identities and built viable states, they resisted the sometimes coercive pull of the Cold War superpowers, while also trying to use them for their own ends. In addition, a new Communist China, established in 1949 and the largest country in the developing world, was deeply entangled within the Cold War contest between communist and capitalist camps. Over the coming decades, however, it would come to act ever more independently from either the United States or the Soviet Union.

During the war, governments had made significant strides in developing new technologies in areas such as aviation, radar, missile technology, and, most ominous, nuclear energy. Scientific and technological breakthroughs achieved in a military context held promise for civilian applications, and thus were poised to contribute to recovery and, ultimately, prosperity. In other fields, it also seemed time for a fresh start. For example, education could be used to "re-educate" members of aggressor nations and further Cold War agendas, but education could also help more people take advantage of, and contribute to, the possibilities of the new age of science and technology.

For several decades after 1945, the Cold War competition seemed to dominate, and indeed define, the postwar world. Driven by ideology, the conflict extended into politics, economics, science and technology, and culture. Geographically, it came to affect virtually the entire world. From our twenty-first-century vantage point, however, it is clear that well before the Cold War's end in the late 1980s, the world had been moving on from the East-West conflict.

Looking back, it appears that, despite divisions—between communist and capitalist camps, or between developed and developing countries—the world after 1945 was growing more and more interconnected. After the Cold War, this increasingly came to be called "globalization." People in many different places faced shared challenges. And as time went on, an awareness of this interconnectedness grew. One response by people in and outside of governments was to seek common approaches, to think and act globally. Another was to protect national, local, or private autonomy, to keep the outside world at bay. Neither usually existed by itself; reality was generally some combination of the two.

Thematically organized, the nine volumes in this series explore how the post–World War II world gradually evolved from the fractured ruins of 1945, through the various crises of the Cold War and the decolonization process, to a world characterized by interconnectedness and interdependence. The accounts in these volumes reinforce each other, and are best studied together. Taking them as a whole will build a broad understanding of the ways in which "globalization" has become the defining feature of the world in the early twenty-first century.

However, the volumes are designed to stand on their own. Tracing the evolution of trade and the global economy, for example, the reader will learn enough about the political context to get a broader understanding of the times. Of course, studying economic developments will likely lead to curiosity about scientific and technological progress, social and cultural change, poverty and education, and more. In other words, studying one volume should lead to interest in the others. In the end, no element of our globalizing world can be fully understood in isolation.

The volumes do not have to be read in a specific order. It is best to be led by one's own interests in deciding where to start. What we recommend is a curious, critical stance throughout the study of the world's history since World War II: to keep asking questions about the causes of events, to keep looking for connections to deepen your understanding of how we have gotten to where we are today. If students achieve this goal with the help of our volumes, we—and they—will have succeeded.

−Ruud van Dijk

Two survivors search for food in a Berlin garbage dump in 1945, after Germany's surrender at the end of World War II.

WORDS TO UNDERSTAND

alliance: nations or groups that agree to cooperate to achieve a particular goal.

devaluation: as used here, deliberate reduction in the value of a nation's money.

fascist: relating to rule by a dictatorship, often promoting national or racial purity.

ideological: concerned with ideas.

obliterated: destroyed completely.

tariffs: duties, or fees, levied by a government on imported or exported goods.

watershed: as used here, like a milestone; highly influential.

CHAPTER 1

A World of Deprivation

World War II had been over for three years, but Berlin was still a city in turmoil. By the summer of 1948, it had become the first flashpoint in the new Cold War, an **ideological** battle between communism and the Western democracies. The United States, Britain, France, and the Soviet Union—the former Allies that had defeated Germany, Italy, Japan, and the rest of the Axis powers—had carved the country into zones of occupation. The four-way partition extended to Berlin, even though it was in the middle of the Soviet sector. Strains in the **alliance** between the West and the Soviets threatened to escalate into an even wider conflict.

Traute Grier, a teenager at the time, remembered those tortuous days well. Germany's economy was in shambles. Coal, food, and other necessities were in short supply. The war had **obliterated** the city's electrical, sewer, and water systems. Berlin's once grand boulevards were reduced to rubble. "I saw how people literally ate the garbage off the streets and desperately tried to fill their stomachs with potato peels and grass," Grier wrote for the German magazine *Der Spiegel* in 2008.

Grier and her mother lived in the American sector of West Berlin, where life was slowly getting back to normal. The Americans provided the Germans with food, energy, and other supplies. Moreover, the Western democracies were slowly trying to revive the German economy, as well as their own, by establishing a free market system, an approach the communist Soviet Union did not support.

On June 25, 1948, life changed drastically for those living in West Berlin. The Soviets closed the door on food shipments by blockading the land and water routes that connected the western sectors of the city to the outside world. It was a calculated move by Soviet leader Joseph Stalin to force the Western powers to retreat from the city.

The blockade was front-page news the next day in the *New York Times*. "About 2,250,000 Germans in the Western sectors of Berlin came face to face with the grim specter of starvation . . . [as] the Soviet Military Administration banned all food shipments from the Soviet-controlled areas into Berlin as part of its calculated policy of starving the people of the Western sectors," the *Times* reported. "Although they see dark days ahead, the Berliners remained calm."

Within days, the Americans and British, along with other World War II allies, began a massive airlift to resupply the city. The airlift lasted for nearly a year. On May 12, 1949, the Soviets finally lifted the blockade, allowing food and other goods to flow freely into the city. The blockade and the Berlin Airlift were **watershed** events that helped lead to the creation of two German states—East and West Germany. For the next four decades, the Western democracies, led by the United States, asserted their liberally minded dominance and capitalist market system over Western Europe, while the Soviets pushed communism in the East. This battle soon raged in other areas, including Africa and Latin America. The result was striking. Countries that subscribed to the free market system of the West fared much better than state-controlled systems. The different economic philosophies had ramifications for the alleviation of poverty and for social development.

Even though economic development was strong in Western, capitalist-leaning countries, communist economic policies advocated by the Soviets attracted many nations in the Third World, especially those that had once been colonial possessions. At the time, the Soviets made a strategic decision to focus their attention on economically developing countries that had been exploited by the colonial powers. By helping to modernize and educate people in these undeveloped regions, the communists hoped to deny the capitalist West vital resources, while making the nations of the Third World communist allies.

Many politicians and people living in these poorer countries had long been exploited by Western colonial powers. In their worldview, communism was a way to throw off the shackles of foreign economic exploitation and create opportunities at home.

IN THEIR OWN WORDS

Traute Grier, Who Lived through the Berlin Airlift

At home we carefully had to plan when we would cook, as we only had electricity at certain times. As a result, it was not unusual that my mother would get up in the middle of the night at 2 a.m. and start boiling some potatoes. To keep them warm she would then wrap the saucepan in newspaper and cover it with a blanket before going back to sleep. The next day we would have potatoes, the following day potatoes with soup and the day after soup with potatoes. We were thankful for what we had.

–From a personal account written for the German magazine *Der Spiegel*.

Children in Berlin, living next to the Tempelhof Airport, playing a game they called "Luftbucks," meaning "air bridge," during the Berlin Airlift in 1948; they are using models of American planes sold in toyshops in the city's western sector.

Florence, Italy, in September 1944, one year after its surrender to the Allies during World War II.

Poverty in War-Weary Europe

The economic situation in postwar Europe was dire. The conflict destroyed entire cities and the industrial production of most countries. Millions had become displaced, with many seeking refuge in strange and unfamiliar countries. Agricultural production vanished, leading to starvation in many regions. Jobs were in short supply.

According to data cited by historian Tony Judt in his book, *Postwar: A History of Europe since 1945*, by 1950 some 25 percent of Italian families lived in poverty. Less than half lived in a house with an indoor toilet. Many villages and towns did not have any public water supplies or sanitation facilities. In West Germany, more than 17 million people were considered "needy" because they were homeless. Even the victorious British continued to ration food years after the war's end. Few Europeans owned a house, a car, or a refrigerator.

The economic situation in the Soviet Bloc was even bleaker. Many nations, including Czechoslovakia, Hungary, and Poland, did not abolish rationing until the mid-1950s, while it continued in Albania and East Germany until 1957 and 1958, respectively. The economic situation was so bad in 1953 that 50,000 East German workers faced down Soviet troops in East Berlin to protest economic conditions. In subsequent years, protests took place in Poland (1956), Hungary (1956), and Czechoslovakia (1968). All demanded economic and political reforms. In most cases, the Soviet military put down the revolts.

New Monetary Policies

The United States was the only nation to emerge from World War II stronger than it had been. Its economy was robust. After the war, America found itself as a bulwark against communism. As some Western European nations, including Italy and France, flirted with communism, many in the West were certain that unless the United States took an active role in rebuilding Western Europe, communism would spread across the continent.

Many also feared that if trade did not increase and new monetary policies were not established, Europe would devolve into mayhem, as it did in the aftermath of World War I (1914–1918). The economic collapse of the world's economies after World War I gave rise to **fascist** governments in Italy, Japan, and Germany, which eventually led an even greater world war twenty years later.

Policy makers in the United States understood the challenges that a new world order would bring long before World War II ended. In 1944, world leaders from forty-four Allied nations, including the Soviet Union, gathered at Bretton Woods, New Hampshire, to discuss the economic future of a postwar world.

Some foodstuffs were still being rationed in Britain in 1953 and 1954 , when this ration book was issued.

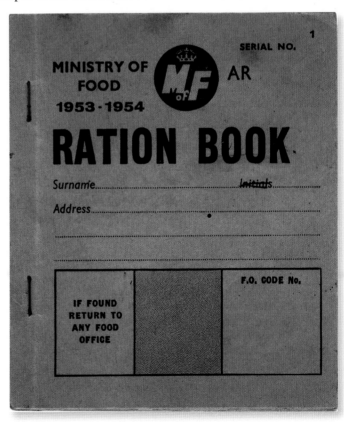

MINISTRY OF FOOD
1953·1954

SERIAL NO.   1

AR

RATION BOOK

Surname.................................... Initials..................

Address...

IF FOUND RETURN TO ANY FOOD OFFICE

F.O. CODE No.

Officially known as the United Nations Monetary and Financial Conference, the goal of Bretton Woods was to provide war-shattered economies with the financial help they needed to rebuild. The guiding principle was the belief that free trade promoted international prosperity and peace. Most of those who attended the Bretton Woods Conference believed high **tariffs**, unfair trading practices, and the **devaluation** of currencies all contributed to the economic calamity that preceded World War II. Several new institutions were formed to aid in the rebuilding effort as a result of the Bretton Woods Conference, including the International Bank for Reconstruction and Development (IBRD), which is now part of the World Bank, and the International Monetary Fund (IMF). While its representatives attended the conference, the Soviet Union refused to ratify the agreements resulting from it, contending that the Bretton Woods institutions favored the U.S. capitalist system.

Workers, ca. 1950, in present-day Gabon, then part of French Equatorial Africa, assembling drill pipes with training, parts, and financing by the Marshall Fund.

Aid from the United States

In March 1948, the U.S. Congress passed the Economic Cooperation Act, originally drafted in June 1947, to provide Europe with $12 billion. Eventually, sixteen nations participated in the Marshall Plan—named after the U.S. secretary of state, George Marshall, who proposed it. They received nearly $13 billion in aid, allowing their economies to grow quickly and helping to stop the communists from expanding westward.

Earlier, President Harry Truman had also offered American aid to help rebuild the Soviet economy and those in the Soviet sphere of influence. Stalin declined the offer and ordered all Eastern European countries not to accept American help. In 1947, in reaction to the original development of the Marshall Plan, the Soviet Union established the Cominform—an international forum of communist parties. Under the Cominform, which had its precedent in the prewar Comintern, the actions of communist parties in Europe were to be coordinated.

Text-Dependent Questions

1. When did the Soviet blockade of West Berlin begin?

2. How long did the Berlin Airlift last?

3. Describe the economic condition in Europe after World War II.

Research Projects

1. Research the founding of the United Nations and write a brief three-to four-paragraph report covering the purpose of the organization, the founders and first leaders, and its earliest activities.

2. Research and write a report on the Berlin Airlift, looking at its causes and its outcomes.

Educational Videos

Berlin Airlift: The Story of a Great Achievement
Page 10
A British Government Public Information Film, produced in 1949, about the joint U.S.-British operation to provide relief to Berliners who were victims of the Soviet blockade.
Published on YouTube by C-SPAN.
https://www.youtube.com/watch?v=ek4tOYKhhb0.

The Candy Bomber
Page 10
A short documentary about Gail "Hal" Halvorsen, a U.S. pilot during the Berlin Airlift, who dropped candy to children in Berlin during the blockade.
Published on YouTube by PBS.
https://www.youtube.com/watch?v=OmanS-4nc4Y.

WORDS TO UNDERSTAND

charismatic: uniquely and powerfully appealing.

guerrilla: relating to a conflict fought by small bands of fighters, not official armies.

imperialism: policy or system of political, economic, and social control by one country or empire over another.

juntas: groups of people who control or take control of a country, usually by force.

nationalizing: taking control or ownership of an industry or company by the government.

ABOVE: The independence monument in Jakarta, Indonesia, shows, on the left, the first president of Indonesia, Sukarno, reading the declaration in 1945 and, on the right, the first vice president, Mohammad Hatta; independence from the Netherlands would not be achieved until 1949, following four years of armed struggle.

CHAPTER
2

Decolonization and Newly Independent Nations

At the end of World War II, the influence of the great colonial powers of Europe was waning. Although many of these countries could barely feed or govern their own populations, most stubbornly held on to far-off colonies in Africa, Asia, the Americas, and the Middle East. During the age of **imperialism**, Europe exploited these colonies for their natural resources and supply of cheap labor. The Europeans also used their colonies as a military firewall against other nations.

In 1945, roughly 750 million people (a third of the world's population) were dependent on the colonial powers for survival. Most European colonies were either governed directly by imperial capitals or through local systems populated by submissive bureaucrats and politicians. After the war, however, a wave of nationalism, a desire for political independence, swept through many colonies. While some European governments granted sovereignty to these territories, others refused to let go.

Each territory's struggle for liberation was unique. For example, the people of today's Indonesia, an island country in Southeast Asia, fought a four-year **guerrilla** war to gain independence from the Netherlands, the oldest colonial power in the region. Elsewhere, Belgium held onto power in its African colonies, while France hung on to its colonies in Africa and in Southeast Asia. Notably, Britain gave up its hold on India soon after the war, in 1947, resulting in two sovereign nations, India and Pakistan.

Some violent independence struggles lasted decades, bred by long-term resentment against the colonizers dating back long before World War II. Such situations often led to strong colonial nationalist movements. For instance, the French occupation of Indochina—including today's Vietnam, Cambodia, and Laos—began in the second half of the nineteenth century; from its beginning, local resistance was strong.

Many nationalistic leaders, such as Ho Chi Minh in Vietnam and Léopold Senghor of French West Africa, now Senegal, were educated in Western schools and were able to deal with their colonial masters as equals. They were also **charismatic**

ECONOMIC BENEFITS AND ECONOMIC COSTS

The Dutch were motivated largely by economics in their struggle to hang on to Indonesia; they hoped to continue to exploit the raw materials of the region, especially rubber and oil, to help the Netherlands recover from World War II. The Indonesian war was bloody, costing the Dutch more than 3,000 military and civilian casualties. In the end, the Netherlands conceded Indonesia's independence.

and were able to put together coalitions that overcame regional, religious, tribal, or other differences. Moreover, each of these countries had developing economies that presented many challenges, including high unemployment and low literacy. In many instances, such as in sub-Saharan Africa, newly empowered leaders enriched themselves while poverty and social inequities persisted for the majority of the population. Long after independence, for many of these new nations, true freedom and economic development have yet to materialize.

The United Nations' Role

The new United Nations was at the forefront in promoting national self-determination. The organization codified its goals in Article 73 of the UN Charter. Among other things, the UN pledged to help people govern themselves by assisting them in "the progressive development

Communist independence leader of Vietnam, Ho Chi Minh, photographed with sailors onboard an East German vessel near the island of Riems in the Baltic Sea in 1957.

of their free political institutions, according to the particular circumstances of each territory and its peoples and their varying stages of advancement."

At its founding, the UN also set up the Trusteeship Council as one of its six main organs, to oversee the decolonization process of what were called the "trust territories." The territories included some dating back to the aftermath of World War I. For example, the region including Lebanon, Syria, Palestine (now including the State of Israel), and Jordan all came under British and French control under the League of Nations mandate system. The United Nations made decolonization and self-determination a high priority. It affirmed that all peoples had a right to independence, including the political freedom to help determine how they were to be governed.

The violence of some independence struggles—often fueled by Cold War, superpower rivalries—would continue into the early years of nationhood for many newly independent countries. Such militarized conflicts would often drain these countries' resources, limiting their ability to address poverty, education, and other development concerns.

Recognizing these challenges, the UN set forth guidelines for establishing economic order in these new nations. It said developing countries should be entitled to control the activities of foreign corporations within their borders and that each nation had a right to ensure that trade was equitable and nondiscriminatory. Prices of raw materials, manufactured commodities, and other exported goods should also be fair. The UN also said that developing countries had a right to adopt economic and social systems that were appropriate for that nation's own development. Despite the fact that the United Nations articulated these objectives in its charter and other critical documents, the practical effects of the mechanisms it put in place were limited.

New Institutions in India

Ninety new countries emerged between the mid-1940s and the 1990s, and some were able to develop the political and economic institutions that they would need to survive. India, for example—one of the largest of these new countries—gained its independence from Great Britain in 1947 through a relatively peaceful, long-lasting independence movement. It formed a parliamentary democracy despite its religious, cultural, and ethnic differences.

At the time of its independence, hundreds of millions of Indians lived in chronic poverty, and by 1951 nearly 50 percent of all Indians lived below the poverty line. Although 70 percent of India's working population farmed, the country was not able to feed itself and did not have enough raw materials for industry. Not only was its economy grossly underdeveloped, but literacy rates were drastically low: the country suffered from an 84 percent illiteracy rate. Some 60 percent of children between the ages of six and eleven did not attend school. Mortality rates were also high.

During the colonial period, the British exploited India's economy, draining its wealth and forcing millions to live in extreme poverty. In the 1700s, India controlled 23 percent of the world's economy, but by 1947 that number had dwindled to just 4 percent. The reason was not hard to understand: India existed for the benefit of Britain. By the 1800s, India had become the biggest buyer of British-made goods, driving many Indian merchants and workers into destitution.

Gandhi, India's nonviolent independence leader, during the Salt March in India in 1930; the protest was one part of the resistance against British rule, particularly against the taxes that Britain levied on Indian salt—a practice that promoted Britain's monopoly on the salt trade.

Jawaharlal Nehru, on the left, with Gandhi in 1947, when Nehru became India's first prime minister following independence from Britain.

When India gained its independence, it tried to solve its intractable economic problems by balancing the role of a free market economy with that of the state. Most small and medium-sized businesses and industries were privately owned, while the government controlled most consumer services, including railroads, airlines, and communications. The government also provided its citizens with social services and education. It began to replace foreign imports with domestic production.

India's first prime minister, Jawaharlal Nehru, expected that this amalgamation of social democracy and Soviet-style planned economy would spark rapid development and prosperity in both the public and private sectors. Just the opposite happened. India's annual growth rate stagnated around 3.5 percent from the 1950s to the 1980s, while per capita income—the average income earned by each person—grew by only 1.3 percent. The number of those living below the poverty line increased from 45 percent in 1951 to 47.3 percent in 1980, according to the Indian Council for Research on International Economic Relations.

It wasn't until India began to liberalize its economic policies in the 1980s and 1990s that the country's economy began to grow. At the time, India's government started to adopt so-called neoliberal economic reforms—that is, those that rely on free markets more than a centrally planned economy. By the 1990s, these neoliberal policy changes were in full swing, although the benefits did not trickle down to many sectors of society. While the government made elementary education a fundamental right, this did not necessarily translate into more educational opportunities. In 1990 and 1991, the government spent 10.4 percent of its budget on education, a number that increased by only 1.0 percent in twenty years. Moreover, the total government expenditure for all social services programs (including education and health, among others) was 20.2 percent in 1990 and 1991. By the end of 2012, it had grown only to 24.0 percent.

The View from Zaire

Although many postcolonial governments were stable, others were ruled by brutal dictators or military **juntas**. Many of these nations also found themselves in the middle of an economic, military, and social tug-of-war between the Soviet Union and the United States. The Cold War struggle caused much political turmoil in many of these newly minted nations, especially in the African nation of Zaire (today's Democratic Republic of the Congo).

In 1960, the former Belgian colony of the Congo achieved its independence, becoming the Republic of the Congo under the leadership of Prime Minster Patrice Lumumba. Although it became an autonomous nation, the Belgians still had a hand in Congolese political and military affairs, which caused widespread political dissatisfaction, even as divisions among the Congolese themselves existed. The army mutinied against Belgian officers, and Lumumba appointed Mobutu Sese Seko as the head of the army.

Lumumba turned to the Soviets for assistance and received a massive infusion of military aid after asking the United Nations for help. The U.S. government, which feared communism would take root in the Congo and elsewhere in Africa, supported Mobutu. The country devolved deeper into political disarray. Mobutu slowly gained control, and Lumumba was then taken captive. Although he escaped, Lumumba was assassinated on January 17, 1961. Mobutu ultimately consolidated his power by staging a successful military coup in 1965. Once he seized power, Mobutu changed the country's name to Zaire and ruled with an iron fist.

For thirty-five years, the Americans turned a blind eye as Mobutu and his political associates stole billions of dollars from the country's treasury after **nationalizing** more than 2,000 foreign-owned businesses. By the mid-1970s, thousands of foreign workers had left the country, contributing to an economic disaster. The plunder was so great that Zaire's infrastructure crumbled. Commerce came to a halt. Even though Mobutu reversed his nationalization order in 1976, the economy never rebounded. Zaire could no longer repay its debt, which led the World Bank to suspend the country's ability to borrow.

A series of civil wars tossed Zaire into more political and military chaos. Tens of thousands escaping a genocidal civil war in nearby Rwanda complicated matters even more as they sought refuge in Zaire. The situation became so dire that Mobutu fled into exile in 1997.

Mobutu Sese Seko, on the left, ruler of Zaire (present-day Democratic Republic of the Congo) in Washington, D.C., with U.S. secretary of defense Caspar Weinberger, on the right, in 1983; the United States supported Mobutu, despite decades of corruption.

Although the new government renamed the country the Democratic Republic of the Congo, Mobutu's plunder and economic policies still reverberated some twenty years after he left. Despite its vast natural resources, which made the Congo attractive to its former Belgian overlords, most Congolese are still trapped in poverty. The Congo's literacy rate is 82.8 percent, while its gross domestic product (GDP)—the total value of all goods and services produced in the country—was $32.69 billion in 2013. According to the World Bank, the country's GDP per capita was $484 that year, while the unemployment rate from 1999 until 2013 averaged 52 percent. Those numbers reached a high of nearly 67 percent in 2000.

Cold War Competition

Zaire's story is a cautionary tale of how Cold War competition made the transition for many of these struggling countries extremely complicated. The United States provided aid packages and technical assistance to build infrastructure projects such as water systems and roads. In Zaire, for example, the United States propped up Mobutu for nearly thirty years because of his country's location in a strategic part of Africa, where Washington hoped to deny the Soviet Union opportunities for influence. The United States also wanted to develop the country's rich natural resources for use in industrial production.

For their part, the Soviets hoped to entice these newly independent countries by highlighting the advantages of a state-run economy and classless society—ideals that clearly had appeal for societies concerned with addressing poverty, education, and other areas of development. The Soviet Union hoped to convince the new governments that communism was a better economic and social alternative to capitalism. It tried to portray its relations with developing countries in benign terms, when in reality the Soviets wanted to exploit natural resources and turn developing countries into allies supporting the Communist Bloc.

Many developing countries refused to be caught in the middle; in the process, the Non-Aligned Movement was established in 1961. The seeds were planted in 1955, when representatives from twenty-nine developing countries in Asia, Africa, and the Middle East met in Bandung, Indonesia, to discuss various economic and development issues. The Bandung Conference, led by the leaders of Indonesia, India, and Egypt, among others, was organized to formulate a set of principles that would guide each country in its relations with the "developed" world. Delegates talked about non-aggression, self-determination, and mutual cooperation and support.

Seen here is the closing ceremony of the meeting of the Non-Aligned Movement that took place in Iran in 2012, fifty-one years after the movement was established and over twenty years since the end of the Cold War.

Text-Dependent Questions

1. Why did the Dutch want to hold on to their Southeast Asian colonies?

2. Which nationalist leader wanted Vietnam to be an independent state?

3. Which African leader did the United States support for nearly thirty years?

Research Projects

1. Create a chart of Africa that shows which nations gained their independence from their colonial masters after World War II. The chart should include the name of the country, the imperial power that ruled the country, the date of independence, and whether independence was achieved peacefully or by war.

2. Pick one of the people mentioned in this chapter and write a biography covering that person's legacy concerning poverty, education, or inequality.

Educational Videos

Mahatma Gandhi First Television Interview (30 April 1931)
Page 20
Said to be the first television interview given by Gandhi; taped by Fox Movietone News.
Published on YouTube by Rareindiaphotos.
https://www.youtube.com/watch?v=dpjBWw5w444.

President Sukarno, Opening Speech at the Bandung Conference, 1955
Page 24
A film of Indonesian president Sukarno's opening address to the heads of state and other representatives from Asia, Africa, and the Middle East who met in 1955 to establish a dialogue among themselves, separate from Cold War superpowers.
Published on YouTube by Timescape Indonesia.
https://www.youtube.com/watch?v=DRIch247vb8.

The construction of the power house for the Norris Dam in 1936, part of the Tennessee Valley Authority's work to provide electricity to this poor region of the country during the Great Depression.

WORDS TO UNDERSTAND

agrarian: related to the land and agriculture.

offensive: as used here, a campaign to promote something or to win a war.

privatization: process of transferring ownership of a public company or industry, such as an electric or phone company, to a private entity.

proletariat: referring to the working class.

regimes: governments.

socialism: system in which the public, through its government, owns and controls a country's property and business operations.

CHAPTER
3

The Cold War and Social Welfare

I n the summer of 1953, U.S. president Dwight D. Eisenhower looked over the political and economic landscape of the United States and saw something that concerned him. Specifically, he was eyeing the Tennessee Valley Authority (TVA), a federally owned hydroelectric power company formed in 1933 under President Franklin Roosevelt. Established as part of the New Deal programs that helped the United States recover from the Great Depression, the TVA provided electricity for thousands of poor people in the Tennessee River Valley.

Eisenhower said the TVA was an example of "creeping **socialism**." When asked at a press conference what he meant by the phrase, Eisenhower explained that he thought it was socialistic to use money paid by all taxpayers and funnel it into a single region in order to attract industry away from other areas. "It seems to me that we have got to have some kind of reevaluation of all these things," he said.

Eisenhower's view that socialism was slowly seeping into the fabric of American political, economic, and social life was not unfounded. When World War II ended, many governments started to implement social programs to protect citizens from economic fluctuations and the uncertainties of life. Even before that, the economic devastation caused by the Great Depression forced many governments, including the United States and Great Britain, to set up programs to aid the sick, hungry, unemployed, and elderly.

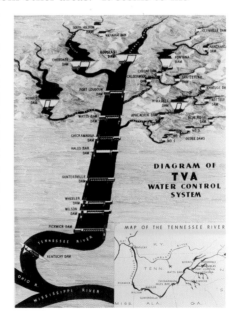

Diagram of the dams designed to produce hydroelectric power under the Tennessee Valley Authority, one part of the New Deal programs of U.S. president Franklin Delano Roosevelt.

Social Welfare on the Rise in the West

After World War II, Great Britain took the lead in transforming itself into a social welfare state, despite the misgivings of Winston Churchill, the leader of the Conservative Party. After the war, those living in Britain were tired of stagnant wages, constant labor problems, pervasive food shortages, and inadequate health care. Clement Attlee, head of Britain's Labour Party, provided a socialistic alternative to Churchill's Conservative government. Although Churchill railed against the social welfare policies proposed by Attlee's party as "abhorrent to British ideas on freedom," voters picked the Labour Party to form a new government in 1945.

A year later, Prime Minster Attlee and his Labour government nationalized Britain's electric, steel, rail, and coal industries, taking

A poster of British coal miners by artist George Bissill, a miner himself, commissioned by the British Ministry of Information during World War II; coal miners benefited from the policies of the Labour government following its coming to power in 1945.

over the means of production and distribution. Any profits made by each industry would now benefit the British people directly. Coal miners, for example, received paid vacations, paid sick time, and better working conditions. The new government in 1948 also established the National Insurance Act, which created the foundation for the British welfare state. The object of the act was to provide British citizens with free health care and adequate income if they lost their jobs, got too old to work, became sick, or became economically devastated by the death of a working spouse. In Great Britain there was a universal belief that government should play a positive role in people's lives, and the National Insurance Act went a long way in fulfilling that goal. The Labour government also tackled other issues, such as rebuilding slums and free education.

However, cracks in Britain's social welfare state began to emerge. As Britain—and most other Western countries, for that matter—transitioned to postindustrial economies and faced competition from emerging economies and rising oil prices, economic hardship was on the rise. By the 1970s, unemployment rates had increased, as did inflation. The cost of welfare programs was draining the economy. During this period, Prime Ministers Harold Wilson, James Callaghan, and Margaret Thatcher cut government spending deeply to rein in inflation. Specifically, Thatcher, who came to office in 1979, focused on reviving the economy by reducing health care and education spending.

Under Thatcher, the government denationalized many industries and reduced the power of trade unions. In Thatcher's view, economies succeeded if government stayed out of people's lives. Thatcher believed that free market competition, private investment, restrained government spending, and **privatization** created strong economies. Thatcher's initiatives shortchanged government support of education and social welfare programs. While many historians say that Thatcher's actions jump-started the British economy, others blame her for doubling the nation's poverty rate.

Social Welfare in the United States

America's social welfare system began in earnest during the Great Depression, as Franklin Roosevelt pushed through Congress his signature New Deal legislation. Roosevelt created forty-two new government agencies designed to create jobs, regulate banks, and enhance the economic security of workers. One of the hallmarks was the Social Security Act of 1935, which aimed to increase economic security for the elderly, a group hit especially hard during the Depression, as well as support for the unemployed.

When Eisenhower entered the White House in 1953, he questioned the wisdom of what Roosevelt had done. But, even though he wanted to limit the influence of government, Eisenhower did not dismantle the social welfare programs that FDR had created. In fact, in many ways he expanded on what Roosevelt had started. For example, he created the Department of Health, Education, and Welfare "to improve the administration of the vital health, education, and social security functions" of the government.

Eisenhower also allowed the government to subsidize farmers, and he even expanded Social Security to benefit more Americans, including the families of deceased workers. He also gave the Federal Housing Administration more money to help more people buy homes. His administration also launched the Interstate Highway System, a massive government program that provided jobs for millions.

In the 1960s, President Lyndon Johnson's Great Society was a watershed program for social welfare in the world's largest capitalist society, even eclipsing Roosevelt's New Deal. The Great Society created dozens of new offices and programs to combat poverty by helping people find jobs, receive an education, and help pay for health care. The War on Poverty program, one aspect of the Great Society, involved a wide range of legislation, including the Economic

Two posters from the late 1930s and early 1940s promoting Social Security benefits put in place under U.S. president Franklin Delano Roosevelt's New Deal programs.

The signing of the Economic Opportunity Act by U.S. president Lyndon Johnson in 1964; it was a centerpiece of the War on Poverty, part of the Great Society initiative Johnson launched during his presidency.

Opportunity Act. This 1964 bill established such programs as Work Study, which supported part-time jobs on college campuses for low-income students.

However, social welfare programs in the United States were attacked under the conservative politics of President Ronald Reagan, who came into office in 1980. Like Britain's Thatcher, Reagan wanted to reduce the size of government, cut taxes, balance the budget, and withdraw support for social programs. Many said these programs, known as "welfare," were creating a "culture of dependency," although supporters dismissed such statements. According to the Ronald Reagan Presidential Library and Museum, his first budget cut $39 billion in social spending, gutting programs used by the poor, disabled, and elderly, even as legislation passed under Reagan aimed to make the Social Security program more financially secure in the long run.

Communism and Social Welfare

The massive destruction caused by World War II presented the communist **regimes** of the Soviet Union and other Eastern European countries with unique challenges as they sought to build up their economies. Communism—essentially an extreme form of socialism in which the means of production are owned by the state and used collectively to enhance social well-being—was put to the test in a variety of ways.

Like the West, the Communist Bloc believed that economic development was essential in transforming their societies. That's where the similarities ended. While Western countries achieved their social welfare goals by using free market institutions, along with targeted government intervention to make markets run smoothly, the Communist Bloc imposed direct state control over their economies. Beginning in the late 1920s under Stalin, the Soviet Union underwent rapid, state-controlled industrialization, transforming the **agrarian** country into a modern economy. The collectivization of farms forced peasants to give up their private farmland, which met with huge resistance. While industrialization and collectivization may have increased employment through the 1930s, World War II changed everything, destroying industrial infrastructure as well as the labor force. After the war, the inefficiencies in the state-run system, the destruction from the war, and the militarization of Soviet society due to the Cold War all had their effects: the economic recovery in the Soviet Union was slower than some of its wartime allies.

With Stalin's death in 1953 and the gradual relaxing of his iron grip on all life in the country, the Soviet economy expanded and was able to absorb more people into its labor force. As a result, the standard of living for many people improved. Moreover, government social programs expanded, including social security that included retirement benefits for the elderly, veterans' benefits, disability and sick leave, and subsidies for low-income families and those with multiple children.

Although communism is, in Marxist theory, supposed to create a classless society, in many ways the opposite was true. Party members in all communist countries had more privileges than ordinary people. Social welfare programs in Czechoslovakia, Poland, and Hungary were unevenly distributed, not only by a hierarchical political rank but also by income. In Bulgaria, for example, health-care funding for farmers and other agricultural workers was much less than for factory workers or government clerks.

By the 1980s, economic development in the communist world had slowed, as a global recession and high oil prices took hold. Indebtedness, corruption, and economic mismanagement placed tremendous pressure on many communist economies. Poverty increased. Using figures provided by the United Nations, historian James Midgley, in his book *Social Welfare in Global Context*, said that by the late 1980s, 24 percent of Yugoslavians lived below the poverty line, as did 22 percent of Poles and 17 percent of Hungarians.

When the economic crisis hit communist countries in the late 1980s, governments began to reverse their social welfare programs as economic production declined. Unemployment soared. Inflation decimated incomes. Poverty rates increased. Homelessness, begging, crime, and utter destitution permeated the communist countries. In Bulgaria, for example, by the 1980s only 28 percent of homes had an inside toilet, and only 7.5 percent had central heating, according to data from *Housing Policies in Eastern Europe and the Soviet Union*.

The Bolshevichka garment factory in the Soviet Union in 1967 in Moscow, where workers produce men's suits; the factory was opened in 1929 by the Soviet state and is still in operation today.

The Role of Education

When the Cold War began, nations began to rethink their educational systems and sought to make various reforms. In the United States, decisions about new courses and areas of study reflected the new political climate. As the space race and arms race accelerated, high schools and universities began to focus on math and science, while schools in Japan and Germany were forced to make changes that were dictated by the nations that defeated them during World War II, including the purging of fascist and other nondemocratic ideas from the curricula.

Discussions about educational reform were influenced by either a capitalist or socialist view of the world. In the Western democracies of France and Italy, for example, communist educational reformers wanted schools to become more secularized, cutting direct links with the Roman Catholic Church in the curricula they taught. They also wanted schools to do away with what the communists saw as elitist admission standards. But the conservative governments in these countries, which were allied with the United States, balked at implementing any socialist or communist reforms.

On the other hand, communist regimes promoted education mostly for political and military reasons. They used schools and universities primarily to establish and promote allegiance to communist ideology. In Cuba, for example, Fidel Castro, whose socialist revolution overthrew the regime of U.S.–supported Fulgencio Batista in 1959, used the nation's educational system to strengthen support for his view of communism.

CUBA'S YEAR OF EDUCATION

Cuba's communist regime placed a high price on literacy. In 1961, soon after the Cuban Revolution, the government's "literacy brigades" began building schools, training teachers, and teaching the illiterate to read and write. It was dubbed the "Year of Education." Factory workers even got into the mix, holding classes for coworkers who could not read or write. Tens of thousands of people traveled to rural areas to teach farmers in small villages. "You will teach, and you will learn," Castro said. He had hoped to reduce the country's 42 percent illiteracy rate down to 4 percent.

Pictured here is a public school in the old part of Havana; improving literacy and public education became cornerstones of Castro's policies after he seized power in Cuba in 1959.

Upon seizing power, Castro closed all the private schools run by the Catholic Church. He also made education universal but geared course study around the needs of the state. Castro made sure students worked on farms or tended gardens at their school as well as going to class. He ordered that anyone who attended school would have to promote his policies after finishing their education. Students were also required to take government-approved courses that championed socialism. Engineering and technical education took precedence over other courses of study, in keeping with the Cold War focus on scientific and technical skills. By the end of 1960, more than 30,000 Cuban students attended technical schools, while another 40,000 attended Cuba's universities. As a result, Cuba's literacy rate, which stood at 56 percent in 1953, improved dramatically, to 100 percent in 2012.

Education as a Weapon

As communism spread across Asia and Eastern Europe and the nuclear arms race took center stage, the United States and other Western democracies readjusted their educational curricula to counter the growing communist threat. That threat came into clear view in 1957, when the Soviets launched Sputnik, the first human-made satellite, into Earth orbit. Sputnik changed how the United States and other nations looked at education. Many believed the educational system of the United States lagged behind that of the Soviets. Politicians bemoaned that American schools did not focus enough on science and mathematics. As a result, the federal government allocated more money to school reform. In 1958, it passed the National Defense Education Act to help strengthen the U.S. educational system at all levels. Great Britain changed its curriculum to focus on international economics. In the Soviet Union and Eastern Europe, schooling focused on math and science.

Education became another strategy in the Cold War playbook. In the United States, one aspect of the 1958 National Defense Education Act targeted colleges and universities, offering them money to enhance their foreign language curricula, as well as their programs in science and math. It was thought that, to aid the United States in the Cold War, more people should be fluent in languages of other countries. In the same vein, a specific section of the Higher Education Act of 1965 funded the development of what are referred to as "area studies" programs, which would help colleges and universities groom specialists in regions, especially those important in the Cold War struggle.

In the developing world, education was an important weapon, as the two main Cold War protagonists tried to steer these countries into their particular sphere of influence. For example, the United States provided students from Africa scholarships to study in the United States. The U.S. and British governments, along with private groups such as the Ford and Rockefeller Foundations, also gave their

African allies money to expand higher education. While the stated reason to help these nations was to build up their educational systems and foster better economic and social conditions, most of the aid promoted prodemocracy ideology.

For their part, the Soviets gave African students scholarships to study in the Soviet Union. The Soviets also built technical institutions in a number of countries, such as Ghana and Ethiopia. Soviet professors and lecturers also visited African countries.

Educational Reform

By the 1980s, reform was in the air. Communism was failing. Reformers such as Mikhail Gorbachev in the Soviet Union began to loosen the rigid control of the state over education. Countries in the West also undertook reforms, aiming to transfer decision making about curricula and organizational issues to local levels. Generally, activists as well as educators pushed to make curricula more relevant and responsive to the real-life needs of students. In the United States, for instance, the government gave states, communities, and parents more choice in school matters. Also, increased choices and private decisions came to take precedence over centrally run systems in many countries in Europe, including Britain and Sweden.

China, the world's largest communist state, also began to reform its educational system. When Mao Zedong and the communists took control of China in 1949, the goal of education was to promote the idea of "serving the people" and "**proletariat** politics." Like its communist counterparts in other nations, the Chinese government had a strong hand in dictating policy. Ideology was stressed over technical and professional competence. When Mao died in 1976 and Deng Xiaoping took power, the government began to improve its educational system as well as its economy, which went hand in hand with China's opening to the outside world. In order to modernize, the Chinese improved training for scientists and engineers. As a result, the government transitioned its educational policy. Colleges and universities were given broad power to choose their own curricula and decide how money was to be spent.

Mao Zedong as he proclaimed the establishment of the People's Republic of China, when communist forces took control in 1949.

Economic Struggle in the Third World

When the Cold War began, many developing nations were impoverished, leaving openings for the United States and the Soviet Union to exploit. In 1958, Soviet premier Nikita Khrushchev began an "economic **offensive**" in the Third World, where he promised to increase industrial and agriculture production and use it as a "battering ram with which we shall smash the capitalist system." The United States responded by increasing loans, grants, and aid to the developing nations. The United States instituted such programs as the Peace Corps and the Alliance for Progress as ways to lift those in the developing world out of poverty. Moreover, it was during this time that some developing nations began to enter into various trade and economic agreements with one another to bolster their economies. Two of the first were Association of Southeast Asian Nations (ASEAN), established in 1967, and the Central American Common Market (CACM), established in 1961.

Venezuela's president Rómulo Betancourt and U.S. president John F. Kennedy (standing at the microphones) at the La Morita Resettlement Project, just west of the capital of Caracas, during a 1961 meeting of the Alliance for Progress.

As the Cold War wore on, economic development in many Third World countries increased, although those benefits did not necessarily pass down to the population. Other developing countries recorded low rates of economic growth, causing or prolonging widespread poverty and deprivation. According to the World Bank, in the 1980s, four decades into the Cold War, the poverty rate for the developing world (minus China) stood at 40 percent.

Some countries, such as Brazil and Argentina, had more success in lifting people out of poverty than other countries. At the end of World War II, for example, Brazil's industrial capacity and transportation infrastructure was old and obsolete. By the late 1960s, Brazil had become the developing world's "miracle economy." Once ruled by a military regime, Brazil started to transition back toward a democracy and institute economic reforms that pushed its economy along, despite some setbacks.

Certain developing countries in Asia—for example, the "Asian Tigers," such as Taiwan and South Korea—had also evolved into economic successes, a process begun in the late 1960s through rapid industrialization. And with the economic transformation of China, the failure of the communist model, and pressure from the IMF and World Bank, many others were poised to emulate their example.

Religious education at the Jamia Masjid mosque in Srirangapatna, India, in 2007.

Growth of Religious Education and the Madrassa

The emergence of independent nations in the postwar world, along with the creation of Israel in 1948, altered the role and significance of religious education, especially in the Middle East. New states began to use education as a tool for political goals, as well as a means of social development and advancement. Israel, for example, used religion and education to enforce the Jewish character of the new state, helping it in its nation-building process and to create political, economic, social, and military institutions. And some Muslim groups used religion and education to further Islamic ideals and enhance nationalistic affiliations.

For Muslims in the Middle East and Asia, Islamic schools called madrassas have long blended religion and education. The madrassa provided students with food, lodging, and free schooling. The schools were formed to prepare Islamic scholars. During the early 1900s, the schools fell out of favor with many Muslim students as they began to attend secular institutions.

However, by the 1970s, the madrassas revitalized themselves by blending religion with politics. This transition was fueled by frustrations in the Muslim world with Western and communist models for modernization, as well as anger at the humiliation of the Arab countries by Israel in the 1967 Six-Day War. Adding to the political and social grievances was the rising availability of money from oil sales in the Middle East, which could be used to finance the development of religious institutions. By the 1990s, many in the West looked upon these schools as breeding grounds for radical Islamic terrorists. That suspicion was fueled after the terrorist attacks on September 11, 2001, when it became known that several Taliban leaders and al-Qaeda members had developed radical political views at madrassas in Pakistan.

Text-Dependent Questions

1. What was the TVA?

2. What was the importance of the National Insurance Act?

3. How did the Cold War significantly change education in the communist world?

Research Projects

1. Research and give an oral report on either President Franklin Roosevelt's New Deal or Lyndon Johnson's Great Society.

2. Research and create a list of at least five social welfare programs created by Great Britain. Give a brief description of each program. What can you conclude?

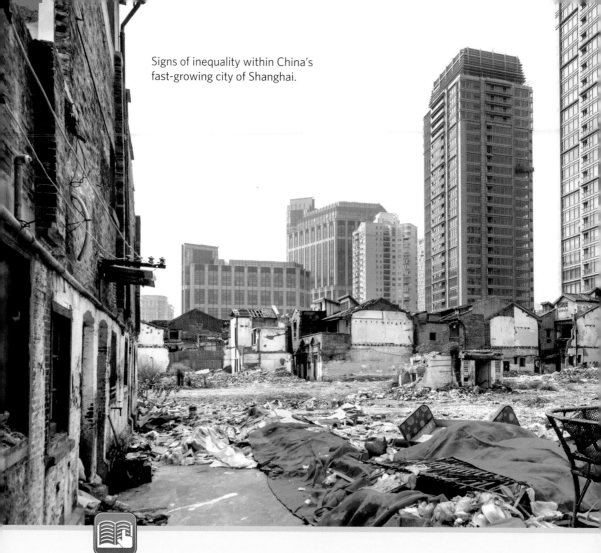

Signs of inequality within China's fast-growing city of Shanghai.

WORDS TO UNDERSTAND

diversifying: making more diverse or varied.

equitable: equal.

grassroots: originating and operating at the local level.

neoliberal: relating to a political view that emphasizes that minimal government is essential for economic growth.

relevant: important; worthy of being noticed.

stagnation: slow or no economic growth.

The Global North and the Global South

During the Cold War, countries aligned themselves according to ideology. The East, for example, included the communist countries of Eastern Europe and China. The West included the United States and its allies.

The world further splintered into First, Second, and Third World countries as the Cold War progressed. The First World came to refer to the industrialized capitalist nations aligned with the United States; the Second World to the industrialized communist states allied with the Soviet Union; and the Third World to the "developing" nations caught between the First and Second Worlds.

Global North and South

In the 1980s, another classification emerged: Global North and Global South. The division between Global North and Global South made its debut when a commission headed by Willy Brandt, the former chancellor of West Germany, ignored Cold War ideology and looked at the economic differences between the richest and poorest nations. Brandt was concerned that the world's economic systems were to blame for poverty and other problems. The terms developed by the Brandt Commission provided social scientists, politicians, social geographers, economists, and others with a new way of assessing the political and economic disparity between societies.

Global North and Global South categorized nations based on industry, political stability, and overall economic development. The "Brandt Line" separating the "Rich North" from the "Poor South" ran in the Americas between Mexico and the United States, then north of Africa, India, and China, and finally down south of Australia and New Zealand. The Global North therefore included the wealthy nations of North America, Europe, and parts of East Asia, such as Japan, while the Global South represented the more impoverished nations of Latin America, Africa, western and southern Asia, and China.

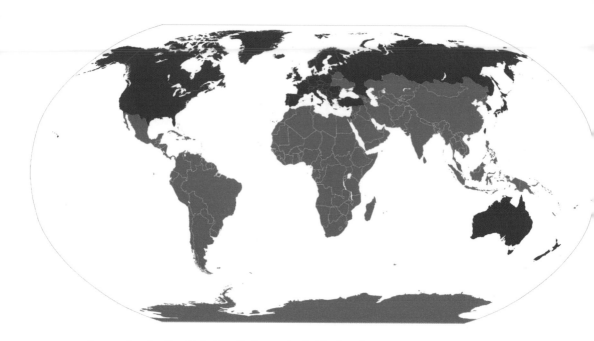

A map showing the Global North (countries in blue) and
the Global South, roughly divided along the Brandt Line.

When the commission finished its work, it called for a series of changes to the global economy in order to make it more democratic and **equitable**. The commission said many of the programs created after World War II, such as the World Bank and International Monetary Fund, did not adequately represent less-developed nations. The commission also said that developing nations were so economically dependent on developed nations that it fostered political instability across the globe. The Brandt Commission envisioned a world where poor countries would have an equal say in global economic solutions and policy making. The commission's recommendations were never acted upon, mainly because of Cold War suspicions and a lack of political will.

Yet the terminology—along with ideas on how to address global poverty and inequality—persisted. The commission's Emergency Program, for instance, included recommendations to address ingrained problems like poverty and hunger. While not acted on, the recommendations stayed alive in the international community and were incorporated at the turn of the century, twenty years after the *Brandt Report* articulated them, and ten years after the end of the Cold War, in the UN's Millennium Development Goals (covered in detail below).

The *Brandt Report* did little to change the mindset of the most developed nations concerning a reapportioning of the world's economic power. Despite the report's recommendations—and in the face of growing **grassroots** activism against economic globalization, the WTO, the World Bank, and other global economic institutions, the countries of the Global North continued to dominate the world's economic discussions in 2015. While emerging markets in the Global South have begun to add their voices to the mix, full integration into the most powerful global institutions has yet to be achieved. One such step—the selection of a leader from the developing world to head the International Monetary Fund—has been pushed for some time, but not yet acted on.

One way the Global North controls the world's economic affairs is through the so-called G7, or Group of Seven. The G7, established in 1976, is a forum of the world's seven most industrialized economies (France, Germany, Italy, Japan, United States, Canada, and Great Britain). They meet periodically to discuss world economic issues. There is evidence that this dominance is changing, however. In an attempt to expand global economic power and address concerns that it remains **relevant** to the changing world economy, the G7 established the G20 in 1999. This larger group includes the major Western countries, as well as the chief emerging economies, such as China, India, Russia, Brazil, and Saudi Arabia, among others.

This hasn't eliminated problems, however. Many critics say that the economic issues highlighted by the Brandt Commission have grown increasingly worse over the years. Pushed along by a number of factors, including globalization, migration, environmental pollution, quality of health care, and quality of education, inequality between the developed and developing worlds persists. Due to free trade rules that allow powerful corporations based in the North to operate across national boundaries, the Global North—to a large extent—still controls international trade and often dictates how technology, foreign aid, and private capital are invested in the Global South. That said, powerful economies in China and South Korea, for instance, are no doubt changing the dividing lines that define the Global North and Global South.

IN THEIR OWN WORDS

Willy Brandt, Former Chancellor of West Germany

At the beginning of a new decade, only twenty years short of the millennium, we must try to lift ourselves above the day-to-day quarrels (or negotiations) to see the menacing long-term problems. We see a world in which poverty and hunger still prevail in many huge regions; in which resources are squandered without consideration of their renewal; in which more armaments are made and sold than ever before; and where a destructive capacity has been accumulated to blow up our planet several times over.

–From the *Brandt Report*, 1980

The Third World Moves Forward

While some countries in the Global South struggled during and after the Cold War, others, including China and Brazil, slowly prospered. China was able to shake off the failed economic programs of Mao Zedong after his death in 1976. Within a few years, China moved to a centrally planned economy that had aspects of capitalism. The country steadily built up its industry, allowed private enterprise to develop and thrive, and began exporting products around the world, while shutting down many of its state-run factories. The government also allowed foreign companies access to the Chinese market. By 2010, China had become the world's largest exporter of goods and the world's second-largest economy, behind the United States, and millions of Chinese were lifted out of poverty.

Other countries in East Asia also had success. Taiwan, Hong Kong, Singapore, and South Korea were able to modernize and industrialize, which allowed their economies to grow. South Korea, in fact, grew the fastest of any country in the world from the 1960s to the 1990s, according to the International Monetary Fund's *Economic Growth Rates of Advanced Economies*. Its GDP per capita in 1980—about $2,300—was only one-third of its wealthier neighbors in East Asia, including Hong Kong and Singapore, but it had climbed to $30,00 by 2010. South Korea made these strides largely through focusing on education, and it now has one of the world's most highly educated technology workforces.

China's huge economic growth has been fueled by international trade; seen here is one of its container ships leaving the German port of Hamburg in 2014.

Brazil's minister of social development and hunger alleviation, Patrus Ananias, discussing the country's antipoverty program called Bolsa Familía in 2009.

Many countries in Latin America also achieved some measure of economic success. While efforts to expand education have been effective, exporting natural resources is a source of income for the region. However, despite economic growth in Latin America, poverty remains a major issue. Some 80 million people in the region are classified as living in extreme poverty. Nearly 30 percent of the region's population has no access to basic sanitation.

Some countries have had more success in lifting people out of poverty than others. Brazil, for example, instituted new reforms in the 1990s. It abolished state monopolies and eliminated trade barriers, accommodating itself to the economic **neoliberal** policies pushed by countries of the Global North. These programs allowed the economy to grow after years of **stagnation**. Coupled with a $6 billion antipoverty program, Brazil eventually became one of the world's emerging economies. Brazil's growth was also fueled by the commodities it exported and government spending that lifted millions of poor people into the middle class. Brazil is now the leading industrial nation in Latin America, the second-largest economy in the Western Hemisphere, and one of the largest economies in the world, ranking seventh in 2014. The rise of Brazil's middle class is one of the hallmarks of its success as a leading emerging economy. According to some estimates, 40 million poor people have made it into the middle class, overall poverty has been reduced by 89 percent, and the unemployment rate has been lowered to just under 5 percent. The country's commitment to addressing poverty includes regular increases in the minimum wage.

That said, Brazil's economy slipped into recession late in 2015. A growing exporter of oil, Brazil's economic troubles stemmed from a global drop in oil prices, which began in 2014. Also, as a major exporter to China, Brazil's economy has suffered as China's economy has slowed down. The uneven performance of the Brazilian economy is a cautionary tale about the overreliance of developing economies on commodities such as oil. These countries recognize the importance of **diversifying** economic life to help cushion their people from globalized slowdowns.

A meeting of Mercosur (or Mercosul), a trading bloc in South America, in 2005.

Learning from early successes with regional trade agreements, Brazil also teamed with several other South American countries, including Argentina, Paraguay, and Uruguay, in a common economic market called Mercosur. The group aims to promote growth through trade, including elimination of tariffs, making it easier for these nations to trade with one another.

The Growing Role of the United Nations

Soon after it was founded, the United Nations began working to help underdeveloped nations create their own solutions to their specific development and economic needs. When the United Nations Development Programme (UNDP) launched in 1965, following the merging of two previous UN agencies, it became the UN's main development network. Its goal was to help countries connect to resources that would improve people's lives.

In the 1970s and 1980s, following the ideas of Indian economist and philosopher Amartya Sen, the UN began to adopt a fuller approach to development, expanding it to encompass not just economic growth, but also the increased capacity of people to satisfy their needs and desires. In 1990, the UNDP published its first *Human Development Report*, disseminating this fuller model of development and poverty reduction. As the turn of the century approached, the UNDP developed a series of Millennium Development Goals (MDGs) to combat poverty, hunger, disease, illiteracy, environmental damage, and discrimination against women. The eight MDGs were designed to be both measurable and achievable.

Text-Dependent Questions

1. Name three countries each in the Global North and the Global South.

2. What was the Brandt Commission?

3. Do most people in the Global South live in cities or in rural areas?

Research Projects

1. Break off into two groups of five or six. One group will represent the Global North, the other the Global South. Research the various issues facing countries in both categories. Debate and negotiate an economic treaty that you believe will help the economies of both grow. In your negotiations, discuss ways to increase trade, improve education, and reduce poverty.

2. Imagine you are the owner of a car company. You want to open a new factory, and you think you should open it in a foreign country because costs will be lower. Before you do so, you need to test that theory. You have to take into account such costs as labor, transportation, materials, taxes, and real estate—including projects into the future. Research two or three countries in the Global North and the Global South and decide the best place to build your factory. What influenced your decision? Discuss your findings with your class.

A scene from the India
International Trade Fair in 2008.

WORDS TO UNDERSTAND

elites: groups with special privileges.

environmental sustainability: processes that are beneficial for and help to
promote the long-term health of the environment.

integrated: relating to a functioning or unified whole.

manifestations: ways of showing or representing ideas or trends.

phenomenal: extraordinary.

CHAPTER
5

Today's Globalizing World

Globalization helps nations use technology, communications, and transportation to connect with each other culturally, politically, and economically. Since the end of World War II, two views of globalization have emerged. The first, put forth by many economists, posits that increased trade and economic activity between nations lift people out of poverty. The second paints a grimmer picture. In this analysis, globalization allows rich nations to exploit less-developed countries, creating an ever-widening economic breech between rich and poor.

Whichever view one subscribes to, globalization is a messy business. The rapid pace of change in recent years seems to have left many people—from the newly unemployed in the United States or Great Britain to those living in extreme poverty in sub-Saharan Africa or South Asia—beyond the promise of an increasingly **integrated** world economy.

Digital Revolution, Digital Divide

The emergence of the Internet, along with cell phones and other forms of digital technology, has made it easier for people to receive and share information. The so-called digital revolution has increased cooperation among nations and allowed many businesses to expand and generate greater profits. Digital devices, such as computers, smartphones, and tablets, allow access to educational opportunities. Information technologies also drive wealth creation, while increasing productivity and competitiveness.

However, many people in developing countries do not have the same access to digital resources as those in industrialized societies, creating barriers to global economic integration as well as economic growth in the Global South. In 2014, the World Economic Forum released its thirteenth annual *Global Information Technology Report*. The report concluded that the digital gap between developed and developing nations showed no signs of narrowing. According to the report, no nation in the Global South was ranked in the Top 20. The disparity magnifies the existing socioeconomic problems the Global South faces.

Income Inequality

Just as technology is uneven across countries and regions, so too is income and wealth. For many countries, as globalization has expanded, poverty has increased and incomes have decreased. According to Nancy Birdsall, director of the Economic Reform Project at the Carnegie Endowment for International Peace, at the end of the nineteenth century the ratio of the average income of the richest to the poorest country was 9 to 1. In other words, the richest country at that time was nine times as wealthy as the poorest nation. Some fifteen years into the twenty-first century, that ratio is more than 60 to 1. In short, the wealthiest nations—the developed, industrialized countries—have gotten a lot richer, while the poorest countries have stayed poor, marking a severe rise in worldwide income inequality.

Income inequality occurs and can be measured both within a country and between countries. It has become a serious issue for many nations. China's **phenomenal** growth rate has led to major income disparities between city dwellers and those living in rural areas. In India, according to Credit Suisse Research Institute statistics cited by the *Hindu* newspaper, the wealthiest 10 percent steadily accumulated more riches during the early 2000s, controlling just over 65 percent of India's wealth. By 2014, that number had climbed to 74 percent.

In the United States, the income gap has shrunk the middle class, while the ranks of the rich and the poor have increased. According to the Pew Research Center, in 1971 some 14 percent of Americans were in the upper-income category. In 2015, that number was 21 percent. (The upper-income tier is defined as a three-person household earning at least $126,000 a year.) Concurrently, 25 percent of U.S. households were part of the bottom tier of wage earners in 1971. In 2015, that number grew to 29 percent. (The bottom tier is defined as a three-person household earning $42,000 or less a year.) Moreover, from 1971 to 2015 the American middle class shrank from 61 percent to 50 percent.

Income inequality is a major problem in sub-Saharan Africa, one of the poorest regions in the world. When it achieved independence from Great Britain in 1966, for instance, Botswana (formerly Bechuanaland) was one of the world's fastest-growing economies, but that growth has not improved the economic life of most of its citizens. Its poverty rate, according to the World Bank, is slightly more than 19 percent, with extreme pockets of poverty in rural areas. The disparity between the rich and the poor is the third highest in the world, right behind South Africa, one of the world's emerging economies with its rapid rise in industrial growth and business opportunities. In South Africa, despite a growing economy, more than 47 percent of the population remains poor, up from 45.6 in 1994. In the summer of 2015, the country's unemployment rate was 25.5 percent. Nearly 25 percent of all South Africans receive government welfare checks.

Income inequality makes poverty insidious in both developing and industrialized societies. Lack of opportunity can lead to a loss of faith in social order. It can lead to political unrest and instability. The Arab Spring, uprisings in several Middle Eastern countries starting in 2010, for instance, was in part motivated by poverty and unequal opportunity. In the United States, the Occupy Wall Street movement sprang up in 2011 over rising inequality due to, according to the protesters, economic globalization and corporate power and greed.

A homeless person asleep on the sidewalk in New York City; homelessness is a persistent problem in many U.S. cities, though the problem has grown in suburban and rural areas as well.

Extreme Poverty

Poverty was a gnawing issue at the end of World War II. The war had devastated much of the world. Millions were homeless and jobless. Many died from starvation because there was little food to eat. Dealing with the devastating poverty and deprivation resulting from the war became one of the primary jobs of the new United Nations as the victorious Allies tried to rebuild Europe and Asia.

Poverty was a major problem not just because of the war. In much of the Global South, it appeared to be endemic, resulting in (and from) chronic social problems, such as illiteracy and lack of education, poor health, and insecure livelihoods. Also,

the independence newly granted to former European colonies in Africa and Asia, while promising great freedom, posed huge challenges to countries that lacked institutions to address social concerns.

The general postwar economic recovery—across the world—came to have its effect, even though progress was slow and gradual. As national economies recovered, trade and investment increased—advances that would, in many cases, eventually trickle down to those most in need. The United Nations made poverty in developing countries a priority. And the poorer nations themselves increased their ability to address the conditions of chronic poverty.

A squatter camp in 2012 in Germiston, South Africa; over 45 percent of South Africans live in poverty.

Economic growth in the Southeast Asian country of Vietnam can be seen in this aerial photo of Ho Chi Minh City in 2016.

MODELING POVERTY

Measuring poverty is a tricky business. Groups that do such things, including the World Bank, take into consideration a number of indicators, such as gross domestic product, meaning the amount of goods and services a country creates; inflation, meaning how much the cost of goods and services rises; per capita income, meaning the total income of a country divided by total population; and complex models that measure income equality.

By 1981, according to the World Bank, sixteen years after the UN Development Programme was established, 44 percent of the world's people were living below the global poverty level, and by 1990 that figure was 37 percent. By 2015, 10 percent were living at or below the global poverty rate of $1.90 a day. To put these numbers in perspective, the World Bank estimates that 896 million people lived on less than $1.90 a day in 2015, compared with 1.95 billion in 1990 and 1.99 billion in 1981.

The most dramatic reduction has occurred in South Asia, where in 1981 a reported 80 percent of the population lived in poverty. That number dropped to 7.2 percent in 2012. China was the single largest driver of the decline, as more than 753 million people moved themselves up the economic ladder, beyond the $1.90 threshold, from 1981 to 2011.

The Millennium Development Goals

By the end of the millennium, however, it was apparent that poverty—in all its manifestations—was still entrenched in many areas. In 2000, world leaders met at the United Nations Millennium Summit to address these issues in a fresh way. They adopted a set of global development goals to combat poverty, hunger, disease, illiteracy, environmental damage, and discrimination against women. Known as the Millennium Development Goals, the idea was to address the many dimensions of poverty and development through eight clear objectives:

1. Eradicate extreme poverty and hunger
2. Achieve universal primary education
3. Promote gender equality and empower women
4. Reduce child mortality
5. Improve maternal health
6. Combat HIV/AIDS, malaria, and other diseases
7. Ensure **environmental sustainability**
8. Develop a global partnership for development

In 2015, the fifteen-year mandate for the MDGs ended with some considerable successes achieved. For instance, much progress had been made toward Goal 1, to "eradicate extreme poverty and hunger." Target 1A—to halve the number of people living on less than $1.25 per day—has been achieved in all regions of the world except sub-Saharan Africa. This regional disparity exemplifies how the global community came up short, in that it underlines the problem of global inequality: most of the world's poorest countries are in Africa south of the Sahara, and improving the lives of the people in this region has proven to be the most intractable.

The city of Bremen, Germany, supported the UN's Millennium Development Goals in 2005 with a display in one of its central squares; here, the banner promoting Goal 3, which focuses on gender equality and empowering women, is in the foreground, with others behind it.

Ban Ki-moon, UN Secretary-General

The MDGs helped to lift more than one billion people out of extreme poverty, to make inroads against hunger, to enable more girls to attend school than ever before and to protect our planet. . . .

Yet for all the remarkable gains, I am keenly aware that inequalities persist and that progress has been uneven. The world's poor remain overwhelmingly concentrated in some parts of the world. In 2011, nearly 60 per cent of the world's one billion extremely poor people lived in just five countries. Too many women continue to die during pregnancy or from childbirth-related complications. Progress tends to bypass women and those who are lowest on the economic ladder or are disadvantaged because of their age, disability or ethnicity. Disparities between rural and urban areas remain pronounced.

– From the Foreword to the Millennium Development Goals Report, 2015.

In addition to regional inequality, gender gaps are evident in poverty rates: women are much more likely to live in poverty than men. In Latin America, for example, the United Nations says that the ratio of women to men living in poor households continues to increase. In 1997, that ratio was 108 women to 100 men. In 2012, it was 117 to 100. Part of the problem is that only half of working-age women actually participate in the labor force. Globally, women earn 24 percent less than men, while educated women are unemployed at higher rates than men with the same education.

Beyond the Millennium Development Goals

Recognizing that much more remains to be done, the UN has rededicated itself to the goals set forth in 2000. In the so-called post-2015 agenda, the UN has reinterpreted the MDGs as a set of seventeen Sustainable Development Goals, including objectives relating to environmental sustainability as well as poverty, hunger, literacy and educational access, health, and gender equality, among others. Goals 13, 14, and 15, for instance, relate to "Climate Action," "Life Below Water," and "Life on Land." Under the new program, the UN has also pressed for nongovernmental organizations and grassroots organizations to become more active partners in poverty reduction and sustainable development.

The UN works on poverty and inequality in other ways. It helps developing nations coordinate aid programs on a global scale and also works to reform unfair trade practices—for example, through the United Nations Conference on Trade and Development.

Promoting debt relief is one other crucial aspect of helping developing nations build sustainable economies, and one way the UN does this is through its Multilateral Debt Relief Initiative, part of Goal 8 under the MDG program, which aims to strengthen international partnerships in hopes of facilitating economic growth and stability in poor countries.

Education, Poverty, and Development

Education is central to reducing poverty and inequality. It sustains economic growth and is important to the construction of democratic societies. Education improves people's skills, which in turn improves their incomes and their quality of life. However, extreme poverty can impact a child's ability to get an education. Many communities lack the means to provide even the basics, such as books, pencils, pens, and paper. Many schools, especially in rural areas, lack clean running water and electricity.

In some nations, constant warfare and the threat of violence prevent children from going to school. In 2002 in Angola, for example, 1 million children were unable to attend school because fighting destroyed school buildings and supplies, while also decimating the ranks of teachers.

In addition to warfare, lack of accountability in government has held many countries back, a particular problem in resource-rich, developing countries. For instance, in Nigeria, corrupt **elites** have worked hand-in-glove with equally unaccountable foreign businesses to exploit the country's resources. In such situations, the gains have gone to a few at the top, with meager benefits trickling down to the population at large.

Despite these and other problems, the status of education in developing nations has improved over the last twenty years or so. In 2000, according to the United Nations MDG report, 100 million primary-school-age children did not attend school. That number has since declined to 57 million. In fact, the net enrollment in 2015 in developing regions is 91 percent, up from 83 percent in 2000. In addition, sub-Saharan Africa, one of the poorest regions on the planet, has seen a dramatic increase in access to primary education. In fact, 20 percent more students were enrolled in primary school in 2015 than in 2000.

The literacy rate among those aged fifteen to twenty-four increased globally from 83 percent to 91 percent between 1990 and 2015. Moreover, the ratio between the number of women and men attending school has narrowed. Many more girls were enrolled in school in 2015 than in 2000. In South Asia, the number of girls attending primary school now exceeds the number of boys. For every 100 boys attending school, 103 girls attend. That ratio was 100 to 74 in 1990. Despite these gains, the UN reports that 57 million children of primary school age are still not in school.

Girls in their blue school uniforms pose for a photo in Rajasthan, India; in many of the countries of South Asia, including India, girls now outnumber boys in grade school attendance.

Hope for the Future

Despite grinding poverty and deepening inequality—in both the developing world and wealthy countries—recent achievements relating to the UN–sponsored Millennium Development Goals show that, if firm objectives are set, progress can be made. Many studies point to the role of education in lifting people out of poverty to higher income levels. The middle class, especially in developing regions, has grown tremendously, tripling between 1991 and 2015, according to the UN. Yet progress has been uneven at best, as poverty is overwhelmingly concentrated in only a few nations, and climate change, corrupt governments, and conflict conspire to threaten whatever achievements the world community has made.

"Spurred on by the global mobilization behind the Millennium Development Goals, the world has made extraordinary progress in reducing extreme poverty," UN secretary-general Ban Ki-moon said in 2015. "Ours can be the first generation to witness a world without extreme poverty, where all people—not only the powerful and the privileged—can participate and contribute equally, free of discrimination and want."

Text-Dependent Questions

1. How many Americans currently live in poverty?

2. What was the global poverty rate in 2015?

3. How many people globally lived in extreme poverty (less than $1.25 a day) in 2015?

Research Projects

1. Create a computer slideshow showing the effects of poverty on people in a particular country. Use photos and statistics.

2. Research ways your community combats poverty and create a public-service poster describing what programs are available to the poor.

Timeline

1945	The United Nations is established at the end of World War II with aims to address poverty and education across the world, as well as to ensure peace and security.
1948	The U.S. Congress passes the Economic Cooperation Act to fund the Marshall Plan, providing Europe with $12 billion.
	Britain's postwar government establishes the National Insurance Act, which creates the foundation for the British welfare state.
	The Soviet Union blockades food shipments to West Berlin; in response, the United States and Western countries begin the Berlin Airlift; the blockade ends the next year.
1950	Five years after the end of World War II, poverty persists in Western Europe; for instance, some 25 percent of Italian families live in poverty.
1951	Nearly 50 percent of all Indians live below the poverty line, four years after India gained its independence from Great Britain.
1953	An uprising of 50,000 East Germans takes place, in which workers face down Soviet troops in East Berlin to protest economic conditions.
1957	The Soviets launch Sputnik, the first human-made satellite, into Earth orbit; in response, the United States allocates more money to education at all levels.
1958	The United States passes the National Defense Education Act to help strengthen education after the Soviet Union launched Sputnik into space the year before.
	The Soviet Union promises to help increase industrial and agriculture production in the Third World; the United States responds by increasing loans, grants, and aid to developing nations.
1961	Two years after Cuba's revolution, its "literacy brigades" begin building schools, training teachers, and teaching literacy; the year is dubbed the "Year of Education."
1964	The Economic Opportunity Act passes as part of the War on Poverty, one aspect of U.S. president Lyndon Johnson's Great Society program.
1965	The UN Development Programme (UNDP) launches, becoming the UN's main development network addressing poverty, health, and education, among other issues.
late 1960s	Brazil has become the Third World's "miracle economy," as it moves from a military dictatorship toward democracy and an open economy.
	Developing countries in Asia—such as Taiwan and South Korea—make economic leaps, helped along by rapid industrialization.

1970s	Madrassas, originally schools to train Islamic scholars, broaden their appeal by blending religion with politics.
1976	Mao Zedong of China dies; the country begins to embrace more open economic policies under Deng Xiaoping ; its educational system begins to modernize as well.
1979	Britain's prime minister Margaret Thatcher takes office and focuses on cutting government spending by reducing health care and education costs, among other cuts.
1980	U.S. president Ronald Reagan takes office; like Britain's Thatcher, he aims to reduce the size of government and cut taxes and social programs.
	The terms "Global North" and "Global South" are established to delineate the richest from the poorest countries.
1980s	Four decades into the Cold War, the poverty rate for the developing world (minus China) stands at 40 percent.
	Economic development in the communist world has slowed and poverty has increased, as a global recession and high oil prices take hold.
1990	The UNDP publishes its first *Human Development Report*, with a model for development and poverty reduction based on human capacity and well-being.
1990s	South Korea grows the fastest of any country in the world from the 1960s to this decade.
2000	The UNDP launches the Millennium Development Goals (MDGs) to combat poverty, hunger, illiteracy, and gender discrimination, among other issues.
2010	China becomes the world's largest exporter of goods and its second-largest economy; millions of Chinese have been lifted out of poverty.
2011	The Arab Spring, uprisings in several Middle Eastern countries, spreads, motivated in part by poverty and unequal opportunity.
	The Occupy Wall Street movement springs up in the United States over economic globalization, corporate greed, and rising inequality.
2014	The World Economic Forum's *Global Information Technology Report* concludes that the digital gap between developed and developing nations shows no signs of narrowing.
2015	Despite success in addressing poverty and becoming the world's seventh-largest economy in the world, Brazil's economy slips into recession as world oil prices drop.
	The fifteen-year mandate for the UN's MDGs ends with some successes, but much work is left to be done, especially in certain regions, such as sub-Saharan Africa.

Further Research

BOOKS

Ballard, Nadejda. *Globalization and Poverty*. New York: Chelsea House, 2005.

Steger, Manfred. *Globalization: A Very Short Introduction*. 3rd ed. Oxford: Oxford University Press, 2013.

Wodon, Quentin. *Education in Sub-Saharan Africa: Comparing Faith-Inspired, Private Secular, and Public Schools*. World Bank Studies. Washington, D.C.: World Bank Publications, 2014.

World at Risk: A Global Issues Sourcebook. 2nd ed. Washington, DC: CQ Press, 2010.

ONLINE

Global Issues: "Causes of Poverty": http://www.globalissues.org/issue/2/causes-of-poverty.

United Nations Educational, Scientific and Cultural Organization (UNESCO): http://en.unesco.org/themes/education-21st-century.

United Nations Millennium Development Goals: http://www.un.org/millenniumgoals/.

United Nations Sustainable Development Goals: http://www.undp.org/content/undp/en/home/sdgoverview/.

World Bank: *World Development Report 2016: Digital Dividends*: https://openknowledge.worldbank.org/handle/10986/23347.

NOTE TO EDUCATORS: This book contains both imperial and metric measurements as well as references to global practices and trends in an effort to encourage the student to gain a worldly perspective. We, as publishers, feel it's our role to give young adults the tools they need to thrive in a global society.

Index

Italicized page numbers refer to illustrations

Index (continued)

Photo Credits

Page number	Page location	Archive/Photographer
8	Top	Shutterstock/Everett Historical
11	Full page	Wikimedia Commons/United States Air Force
12	Top	Wikimedia Commons/Ricce
13	Bottom	iStock/Linda Steward
14	Top	National Archives and Records Administration/George Rodger
16	Top	Wikimedia Commons/Gunawan Kartapranata
18	Bottom	Wikimedia Commons/German Federal Archives
20	Bottom	Wikimedia Commons/Yann
21	Top	Wikimedia Commons/Dave Davis, Acme Newspictures Inc.
23	Top	Wikimedia Commons/Frank Hall
24	Bottom	Wikimedia Commons/Sara Rajaei
26	Top	Wikimedia Commons/TVA Web Team
27	Bottom	Shutterstock/Everett Historical
28	Top	Wikimedia Commons/The National Archives (United Kingdom)
29	Bottom left and right	Wikimedia Commons/Franklin D. Roosevelt Library
30	Top	Wikimedia Commons/LBJ Library
31	Bottom	Wikimedia Commons/Yury Artamonov
32	Bottom	iStock/Evgenia Bolyukh
34	Bottom	Wikimedia Commons/Orihara1
35	Middle	Wikimedia Commons/United States Government
36	Top	Wikimedia Commons/Prakash Subbarao
38	Top	iStock/Nikada
40	Top	Wikimedia Commons/Canuckguy
41	Bottom	Wikimedia Commons/German Federal Archives, Lothar Schaack
42	Bottom	Wikimedia Commons/Buonasera
43	Top	Wikimedia Commons/Marcello Casal JR/ABr
44	Top	Wikimedia Commons/Ricardo Stuckert, PR
46	Top	Wikimedia Commons/Rameshng
49	Bottom	Wikimedia Commons/sonyblockbuster
50-51	Bottom	iStock/Henrique NDR Martins
52	Top	Shutterstock/De Visu
53	Bottom	Wikimedia Commons/Tarawneh
54	Bottom	iStock/EdStock
56	Top	iStock/Izabela Habur
Cover	Top	Shutterstock/Everett Historical
Cover	Left	Shutterstock/Komar
Cover	Right	iStock/btrenkel

About the Author and Advisor

Series Advisor

Ruud van Dijk teaches the history of international relations at the University of Amsterdam, the Netherlands. He studied history at Amsterdam, the University of Kansas, and Ohio University, where he obtained his Ph.D. in 1999. He has also taught at Carnegie Mellon University, Dickinson College, and the University of Wisconsin-Milwaukee, where he also served as editor at the Center for 21st Century Studies. He has published on the East-West conflict over Germany during the Cold War, the controversies over nuclear weapons in the 1970s and 1980s, and on the history of globalization. He is the senior editor of the *Encyclopedia of the Cold War* (2008) produced with MTM Publishing and published by Routledge.

Author

John Perritano is an award-winning journalist, writer, and editor from Southbury, Connecticut, who has written numerous articles and books on a variety of subjects including history, politics, and culture for such publishers as Mason Crest, National Geographic, Scholastic, and *Time/Life*. His articles have appeared on Discovery.com, Popular Mechanics.com, and other magazines and websites. He holds a master's degree in American History from Western Connecticut State University.